DNA OF A CUCKOLD - HUSBAND EDITION

Understanding Yourself, Your Angst And What To Do Next

ALLORA SINCLAIR

Cuckoo
Publishing

DNA Of A Cuckold - Husband Edition

Front Cover Illustration by: Stylepics

To my loving husband. You are what real men are made of. You have shown me what true love really is. Thank you for the gift of power, freedom and joy. Without you, I am nothing.

Chapter One

LIVING AS A CUCKOLD

_S_pending valuable time telling you about the history of the cuckoo bird and the origins of cuckoldry is nice, but I am going to assume you already have a firm grasp on what cuckolding is. So you have this book in your hands because you want to know more than what the internet offers. You're hoping for honest and real clarity on a topic that is arguably one of the most distorted taboos on the internet. It would make any man or woman scratch their head, finding it hard to believe it actually works in any context.

I did not design this book to titillate or excite you, but to look at the condition objectively to address as many of the questions and issues my husband and I faced when we entered 'the life'. IT IS NOT FOR EVERYONE. Although cuckolding is the second most used search term in porn, for most it is a fantasy and frankly should remain that way.

I'm not suggesting cuckolding is bad or should be avoided. Quite the opposite, actually. It is the most amazing kind of relationship any two people can enter. Just like you can fantasize about being an astronaut or special forces navy seal, only a small segment of society has all the things necessary to go there - physical stamina, intelligence, courage, insatiable drive, etc.

Proceeding into this life "just because it seems erotic" is a recipe for disaster. The erotic template that most porn uses to represent cuckolding excludes the most important element. The internal psyche and emotions of both the man and the woman (for this book, my focus is only on the heterosexual cuckold). Most pornography usually shows only the most extreme scenarios and excludes everything about the relationship outside the 20 minutes of sex.

They have often referred to cuckolding as the "intelligence fetish". Unlike other fetishes (feet, latex/leather/rubber etc), it all takes place in the mind. I would argue that cuckolding is a fetish as much as homosexuality is a fetish. A true cuckold does not actively choose to live this life. It can be very turbulent, demanding and difficult. Life inside a "normal" sexual relationship is so much easier and often can prove almost as rewarding. However, a cuck is into cuckolding because it's who they are. For those of you that find it exciting but also find other things sexually arousing, it may be a dynamic you fetishize over. There is nothing wrong with experimenting with your significant other. But for the true cuckold, they rarely want to be a cuckold. They simply are born that way.

Cuckolding is also often placed as a sub-genre under the masochism umbrella. The cuck craves humiliation and deprivation of sexual pleasure. This I believe is a much more accurate depiction. Similarly, the wife must have a sadistic side to her persona. If she doesn't derive some pleasure by inflicting emotional pain on her cuck, it will be a short-lived adventure for the couple.

Both Dave (my husband) and I have spent countless hours trying to figure out if we were just fucked or what. Confusion, misinformation, and outright deception seem to be the driving force behind most of the information out there. From encouraging women to start an FLR (Female Led Relationship) that will ultimately lead their man to comply with their hotwife needs, to books that insist there is some uber-magical way you can "make" your wife or husband into a cuckoldress/cuckold. It's scary and sad.

To be crystal clear, cuckolding is by default a female-led relationship BUT, an FLR may not evolve into a cuckolding dynamic. The sexual synergy of cuckolding ALWAYS evolves into an FLR, NOT the other way around.

I hope that this book will try to break through all of this psycho mumbo jumbo and put things right. If you are truly a cuckold, you will have no doubts by the end of this book. It will help guide you through the challenges and make you realize there is absolutely nothing wrong with you. Just like sexual orientation, you were born this way. You can't stop it. You can't change it. You owe it to yourself and your wife to embrace it, and deal with it head-on.

Chapter Two

SELF DIAGNOSIS

⚬

So, the idea of cuckolding turns you on? Do you think that is enough for you to call yourself a cuckold? Not at all.

Cuckolding is as powerful as it is, for a reason. It addresses a plethora of erotic interests. Some get turned on by the idea of seeing their significant other debase and degrade themselves by being sexually promiscuous. This appeals to the closet sadist that poses as a submissive cuck. These individuals also find themselves turned on by just about any/every fallen angel scenario.

Others find cuckolding erotic because they like to watch in real-time and in real life. They are wannabe cucks that are essentially satisfying their interest in voyeurism. Cuckolding may also be of interest as a gateway into the swinging lifestyle. Get the spouse with others and the door is open for you to get some strange, or so you think at some level of subconsciousness.

Although all the above may be true in a variety of cases, the real cuckold's drive is born out of two reasons and two reasons only. One is out of deep love to see his partner have sexual pleasure at a level he can never provide. The other is a deep-seated need to be masochistic. There is no/zero/nada/zip desire to have his wife debased, nor is there any thought of him having sex with anyone else but his wife. She is his goddess, and he wants to please her and only her.

I don't want you to think I'm passing judgement on those who like to degrade or watch or swing. Done with open consent, there is absolutely nothing wrong with any of them. However, they are all activities that are proactively sought after by choice. The impetus behind a true cuckold's mind is not a choice. It's not just what turns them on. It's what they are, deep in their heart and mind. The choice is not theirs to make.

Before you get too far into this book, a very quick acid test to help you figure out if it's just a kink that turns you on or a deep-seated need, I challenge you to pause all porn surrounding cuckolding for 1 month. Yes, you may have a tough time getting off, but try to avoid the unrealistic fantasies painted in the porn industry. Then, after one month, I want you to immerse yourself in the thoughts of your wife being with another man immediately after you have 'satisfied' yourself. Think about how you would feel as she approaches you and smells of another man. But again, only do this immediately AFTER you get off. Does it still seem like something you want? You can't live without? Like this is how things are supposed to be with you and your life? Yes or No? By removing the sexualization of the event away from your headspace, it should shed some light on what your true motivations and needs are.

Next, try to forget about the cuckolding topic. Take some time to reflect throughout your life on the day-to-day stuff. Have you more often than not chosen to do things 'the hard way'? Do you frequently take actions you know will end up hurting you emotionally (as an example, say working way too hard for your boss, but you know it will never go recognized but you do it... well, because)? Would you say you tend to be masochistic with your day-to-day life? Yes or No? If you've answered yes to both of the above and you have taken the time to be true to yourself, then you may very well be a cuckold.

Take comfort that being a cuckold is a true badge of honor. Admittedly, I'm a little biased, but my husband (Dave/davie) is the most amazing man I could ever hope for in my wildest dreams. He has an enormous amount of self-confidence in himself and trust in me. He also puts me on a pedestal that sometimes makes my head float. And (lucky for me) feeling emotional pain is something that helps him make the world feel right.

Being a cuckold is not a choice, just like being gay is not a choice. You are born this way. You can not change it. You have no control over how you feel. You do, however, have a choice in what you do with it. I suspect no one actively wants to be gay. Likewise, no one wants to be a cuckold. To the outsider, it seems wrong, awkward and riddled with pain and emotional turbulence. To the cuckold, it is like living in paradise.

The wonderful world of psychology has deemed cuckoldry as a variant of masochism. This makes sense when you think about it. Remember, cucks not only forgo to the wife sexually. They also like the emotional pain and humiliation associated with it. That being said, every step you take from this point (including telling your wife) needs to be in baby steps. Once you cross this bridge, you can't un-cross it.

Chapter Three

BUT WHAT IF MY WIFE

☿

 o, I'm going to assume you have read the previous unit and you have self-diagnosed that you are a cuckold. The natural knee jerk next question you'll be asking yourself is what the hell are you going to do with your wife? Is she a cuckoldress/hotwife and what if she's not?

Before I go any further, I want to clear up an overused and abused use of the cuckoldress/hotwife terminology. Technically, they are quite different. I suspect many of you want a hotwife but think you're looking for a cuckoldress. A hotwife engages in the same sexual adventures as a cuckoldress and also with the same understanding that the cuck is a loyal monogamous partner. The vast difference happens OUTSIDE the bedroom and the power differential and motivations. Simply put, hotwifing is an activity you do. Cuckolding/a cuckoldress is a way of life that includes hotwifing activities but is not limited to it.

If I'm being honest, I hate to be called 'Mistress' or 'cuckoldress'. It sounds clunky, pretentious, and makes me feel old. Make no mistake, I was born to live my life as a cuckoldress, but I prefer to be referred to as Goddess or Hotwife. I know, I'm contradicting what I just told you, but it's more a heads up that I interchange these two words based on my personal bias.

Hotwifing as an activity usually evolves from a couple that started the path down swinging initially. Again, to be clear, I'm not condemning hotwifing. If it satisfies both people and makes them happy, I say go for it. Also, some hotwifing can shift into a cuckold dynamic, although this is very rare. Cuckolding is rooted at a much deeper level. It comes out of who we are and what we are born to be. Some people discover this side of themselves because it was deeply repressed their entire life and hotwifing was the door. However, usually, one party in the couple wants to end the cuckold dynamic once the power shift to the wife goes beyond the bedroom.

This is the part of the book you don't want to hear. Many books out there promise a "how to make your wife a hotwife" type of guru, top-secret guide book. Bottom-line, it's not possible. Can you make someone gay? Of course not. They are straight or gay, end of discussion. You're a true cuck or you're simply turned on by the idea until you get off, then it's back to normal life. The identical principle is the case with your wife.

You can manipulate her into doing something she genuinely does not want to do, but this is nothing short of abusive. You need to accept her for who she is. Just like you, only a small percentage of women understand, accept, embrace and thrive in true cuckolding. Am I saying they also need to have a 'born that way'/genetic kind of thing as the cuck? I would argue that, yes, it is.

Common sense would tell you, why wouldn't all women want their own cuck? They get to have sex with multiple partners, have their devoted man totally attentive, and worship the ground they walk on. Newsflash, most women have an operating system that runs almost exclusively on submissive mode. Therefore, most women prefer a take charge, alpha type male as their life partner. They want to be a supportive backdrop to their man's life. There is nothing wrong with that. I'm not suggesting that women are weak or less than a man. I'm saying our culture teaches little girls to be submissive and little boys to be more aggressive. It's embedded deep within modern society at almost every level.

For the cuckoldress, it flips this dynamic upside down and then some. She falls naturally into a dominant role, both in and out of the bedroom. Her partner may be very masculine, but she wears the pants in almost all situations. She must have sadism within her persona. They do not teach this. It's just there, or it's not. Not all women like this control. There is a plethora of other legitimate reasons your better half may choose to not want to go down this path. If she is not interested, willing or feels it's not in her DNA, you must accept this and we're done.

Chapter Four

BRINGING IT UP

𝒩o matter what you do, DO NOT do what Davie did with me.

He sat me down and gave me the "we need to talk" approach. My heart was in my mouth, thinking he was about to say he wanted a divorce. Our sex life sucked, so I just assumed it was me not doing things excitingly enough. I mean, I get it. He was nervous as fuck that I would think he was weird and I would judge him. But holy shit, it took me a good couple of days just to take in what he was trying to tell me.

Remember, this is something you have probably spent many years thinking about. You've probably researched the shit out of whatever the internet spits at you, and you know all the lingo (cuck, bull, chastity, humiliation, power transfer etc). Your wife has no idea that such possibilities exist.

Go slow. Go gentle and do not information dump

everything you know about cuckolding. This is a conversation that CAN NOT be fully addressed in a one-time, sit down kind of way. Most importantly, don't go directly to talking about any kind of sexual activity outside the marriage, period.

Your initial approach should try to address the current situation. Your sex life needs to improve. If you're a cuck, you know this is true, so let's just cut to the chase and assume the obvious. Try to see if she agrees. If she is reluctant to admit you don't satisfy her, that's probably for fear of hurting your feelings. That's ok. It means she loves you and cares how you feel.

The tone should be light and fluffy. No heavy 'Oh my God, Huston, we have a problem' kind of talk. Make it fun. If you both never talk openly about your sexuality, it will feel scary at first but it will quickly be clear she will talk or she is a closed case and that this will take many many attempts at conversing before you can speak of what's really on your mind.

Test the waters to see if she has a sexually adventurous side that you've left untapped. If your relationship already dwells in the realm of "kinky", still move into the concept of cuckolding only after you've talked a few times. Start with "let's spice up our sex life"... perhaps we can try some toys? Perhaps you could move into you expressing your desire for her dominating and suggest some role play - like you don't know each other intimately and she is your boss at work. This will ultimately lead to conversations about sex outside the matrimonial constraints. I want to emphasize it leads to conversations, not actions.

After several discussions, you should start to feel some kind of comfort and openness in sharing your kinks. It gets a lot easier. Once you finally reach a point where sex with each other expands to exploring sex outside the marriage, she may be adamantly opposed to the idea of you sleeping with other women. This is when you have the first opportunity to drop the idea that you seeing her with other men is not only acceptable, it's arousing. From there, you have a fairly straight path into a dialogue of cuckolding.

I cannot state it enough that going from ground zero, where you want to look at ways to spice up your sex life, to talking about the wonderful world of cuckolding should not be done in a single dialogue UNLESS you are already into swinging. This is not half as big a step for couples already into an alternative lifestyle. You want to gradually let your wife catch up to you in the realm of non-conventional/kinky. Depending on how long you have already been together, this could feel like you are meeting a different person than the one you have been with for perhaps decades. That is extremely scary. You may learn to discover that your wife secretly wants you to be her daddy in role-play or that she wants to try swinging. Obviously, not your cup of tea in both cases, but now you may realize the traditional and conservative woman you thought she was is not the case.

My point is, be prepared for anything and everything. It may not be what you want or expect. I assure you, she will, at no level, be expecting you to tell her you want to be her little cucky boy and that you would love her to embrace her inner slut.

The end game in all of this is to open the door to your sexuality as a couple. If I'm to be honest, there is a good chance she is not interested or willing to explore living a cuckold life with you. But there is also a good chance it intrigues her, and she will explore it. Either way, having these open mic night discussions on your sexuality is always nothing but therapeutic and informative.

Expect her to both laugh and decline the idea of you being ok with her having sex while you do the dishes and put the kids to bed. Let the idea sit and steep before you open it up to discuss again. Remember, this is going to take time for her to reconcile the idea of it being ok even if it appeals to her. Monogamy is ingrained into all of us from childhood. They teach us anything outside marriage is cheating. End of discussion.

If she says no, with no consideration, still do not give up. It may take several months to several years for her to be okay being a cuckoldress. Whatever you do, do not push her into doing something, only to feed your own needs, at the expense of destroying her own identity.

Chapter Five

WHY WOULD SHE SAY NO?

꧁

She said "no"? After much time to discuss and explore, she has definitively concluded it's just not something she wants you as a couple to engage in. Well, that sucks! Little does she know you have given her The Golden Ticket. So why did she decline the chance to live a life only a few dare to dream of and even fewer live?

The answer is not as straightforward as you may think. It is likely a combination of issues that go back to her self-confidence, the way they raised her as a child, her DNA and the big imperfect world of genuine fear.

Try to imagine your wife just telling you she wants you to sleep with as many women as you can. Beyond the guarantee of a prostitute, one of your first concerns would be, can you even find another woman that would want to sleep with you? If you've been with the same woman for so many years, your search, flirt and score skills have all but died. Likewise, she may fear the prospect of being embarrassed and ashamed if she can't hold the sexual interest of other men. This is real and should not be undervalued. If she suffers from low self-esteem and self-confidence, this will be a real and valid fear.

Going back to my example of you having a free ticket to fuck any woman you want. If your wife told you this, you would instantly begin asking yourself why? You would think you obviously must not be satisfying her because she couldn't care less if you have sex with her. You would begin thinking she must have a hidden agenda. If you can have sex with any woman, she must be permitting this because she wants to fuck other guys. We both know this is not the case for you, but your wife does not.

Another predominant emotion anyone feels when their significant other has engaged in extra-marital sex is jealousy. Yes, for you cucks, this is the crack-cocaine of being a cuck. You feel it's glorious. Massive amounts of jealousy. And you love it. It is an emotional pain that you crave. Your wife does not, in any way, see any side of this as being positive. She will instinctively fear losing you as you rage in a fit of jealousy. To the average man, this is both a normal and expected reaction. Cuckolds are anything but 'normal' by the stereotypical standards of society. If you ask me, they are genuine men. Davie loves when I try to amp up the jealousy. He has a thing for seeing me in pantyhose. Of course, I never wear them unless I'm with my bulls. I make sure of it. It drives him crazy and we both love it.

Socialization and how they have taught us to conduct ourselves. 'Good girls don't do this kind of nastiness'. Disagree all you want. Society raises women to be good little girls and to be submissive, loyal and proper. If they raised your wife in a household that placed high emphasis on this, she is going to object, even if it interests her in every other way. This is a hard obstacle to overcome for most women. 30-plus years of societal programming becomes near impossible to undo. Understand, this is not necessarily how she feels or thinks, but reflects how deeply the years of being told one thing becomes her status quo.

Not surprisingly, the most logical and real objection that your wife is likely to express is the physical dangers that this kind of life can present. Everything from the wide variety of venereal diseases she puts herself at risk in contracting, to the prospect of dealing with a creep that could put her in harm's way. There will be ample opportunities for her to be with men that she knows next to nothing about. Nothing is stopping them from being a potential psycho chicken from hell. If you're not there to protect her, she is extremely vulnerable to her safety.

The good news in all the above is that every one objection mentioned thus far are objections that can be overcome with discussion, thorough vetting of the bulls, and by you openly expressing your reassurance that her fears about your reactions are ill-founded. She may be a cuckoldress but has repressed this side of herself for so long, she does not even know it exists. Given enough time, all these objections/fears are truly surmountable. The bad news, there are two reasons your wife may or may not express that are deal breakers in pursuing cuckolding beyond an ongoing fantasy that only lives in your mind.

The most obvious reason any wife would not want to engage in cuckolding is a very low libido/sex drive, regardless of what partner she is with. Some women simply don't enjoy sex that much. Not because they haven't been with the right guy to push all their buttons. Because they just don't need or want it that much. Perhaps it's a low level of estrogen, progesterone or testosterone? Either way, these women gravitate towards being asexual and sadly, no amount of dialogue or reassurance will make this kind of relationship happen. If your wife falls into this category, she will also not be into any exploration of sexuality beyond her due diligence to get you off. Her need to be satisfied does not exist.

Finally, the single biggest reason any woman would legitimately have little to no interest in cuckolding - she is not a cuckoldress. What? I know, it seems like this makes no sense but bare with me here. Despite everything discussed, there is one key component that any woman must have to want to embrace being in a cuckold relationship. She may love the idea of being with other men, be okay with being in charge of her little cuck boy and even be okay with going against the social norms of being a 'good little girl'. However, the element she requires that you need, that is a match made in heaven for both of you... She needs to have a sadistic side. Just like you need to have a masochistic side. If she does not derive true pleasure in inflicting emotional pain, humiliation and disparity, it will not happen.

Yes, as a couple, you can explore having a cuckold type of sexual encounter or two, but her becoming a cuckoldress in the truest sense of the word will not happen. Being a sadist has an entire suitcase of negative connotations attached to it, but to a cuckold, it is actually the kindest, caring and loving kind of person they could ever hope for. Similar to low libido, if she does not have a sadistic side, cuckoldry will inevitably remain a fantasy or remain in a hotwife context only.

Before I leave this topic, I can not express enough. This is the one area of cuckolding that both davie and I have never come across when we were new to the lifestyle and doing our research. The sadomasochistic element. I try to expand on this component in my companion book for wives. Frankly, without you being a true masochistic and your wife being a true sadist at heart, cuckolding CAN NOT exist beyond an exploration. Perhaps hotwifing is an option, but as I previously mentioned, cuckolding is not an activity. It's a way of life, just like homosexuality. I believe this makes it so magical. To have a life partner that gets you at such a deep level. To have such opposing dispositions that end up being completely complimentary. It is so rare, so special and so damn hot!

Chapter Six

SHE SAID YES!

Oh. My. God! She said "yes"?

Before you do anything. Do not pass go. Do not collect $200. Take a few minutes to remember exactly how you felt at that exact moment when she said "hell ya!" and burn that feeling into your memory as deep as you possibly can. You never want to forget the sheer joy, the happiness, the excitement you felt. Know that you are indeed the luckiest man alive at that moment. The odds of this happening are only marginally better than winning a lottery. Instinctively you know you have found your soulmate at a level you never thought possible up till this point. I tell you to burn it into your brain because it can quickly be forgotten as you journey together into a life that will be bumpy, challenging, constantly changing and deeply rewarding, particularly in the first year or two.

Cuckold angst, hard manual labor, mental and emotional confusion, financial sacrifices and an immediate and growing shift in power from the traditional husband to the wife all lay ahead. Just like it may have taken your wife several months to several years to resolve her desires with her objections with cuckoldry, you too will need a significant amount of time to sort through the life and relationship changes you're undergoing.

Be patient and loving to each other. You have both just metaphorically "come out of the closet" with each other and, as such, you both need to redefine your own identities individually and as a couple. Your wife needs to stop feeling guilty when she tells you she would love to fuck this guy or that you don't have a big enough cock to cut it. Likewise, you need to feel comfortable being put in your place, told your not a 'real man' or when your wife wants to talk to a prospective bull on the phone while you make the dinner and finish folding her laundry. The life you have shared up to this point will cease to exist. It will morph into a completely new and revitalized relationship that veers away from anything you have ever known. I assure you, the result will be so rich and rewarding to both of you. Your communication, openness and love will be exponentially more but understand, this will not happen overnight.

I remember davie and I watching one too many porno's that show the wife succumbing to another man and instantly taking on the role of a dominating cuckoldress with the husband submitting to be her sissified slave, all on the premise of this being their first time. It just does not happen like that. You will both be nervous, awkward, scared even. That is not only okay, it's totally normal. If you did not feel that way, I'd be a little concerned about the health and depth of your relationship.

Think of your wife saying "yes" not as the destination, but rather as the beginning of a life journey. Now the fun begins, but so does real work as a couple. Perhaps the most critically important point that needs to be mentioned here is the moment your wife says she would like to explore cuckolding, you can never ever EVER hold any of her actions against her. Including her openly disclosing her desire to have sex with other men. You solicited this from her. Don't be a douche.

The other essential point here is to not rush the idea of moving forward either. She said 'yes' but so what? Role play, role play, role play. You may convince yourself you're a cuck, you want her to be a hotwife, she fucks another man and you fall apart cause you thought it would be just like the porn you saw last night. NOT!

Chapter Seven

WHAT YOU NEED TO DO NEXT

❀

*A*ll relationships have their own unique and independent dynamic. Cuckolding is no different. It does not come with a rule book or set of guidelines on what needs to be done or how. Assuming you have both agreed that some form of cuckolding is a direction you would like to explore or perhaps incorporate into your marriage, you both need to lay all your cards on the table.

You've come this far. To suddenly clam up for fear your wife may judge you is silly. If you don't want her to kiss other men during intimate moments, you need to say something. If she finds the prospect of seeing you wearing her panties as a turnoff, don't expect that to happen even if it turns you on. If she loves the idea of using a cock cage to enforce chastity and you think it would be awesome, then say something.

You need to develop a set of boundaries that will make

you both comfortable while you travel down this uncharted territory. As you develop and grow as a cuckold/cuckoldress, you will both begin feeling more comfortable in areas you did not at first. Likewise, you may discover things you think are ok now but may need to be discussed and taken off the table if it makes either of you uncomfortable or upset later on.

Most cuck's love SPH (small penis humiliation). They love to be told how inadequate they are in size, thickness, rigidity or usually, all the above. Every time I tell my davie I only want him to please me orally cause his little pee pee is nothing but frustrating, he gets as hard as a rock. It's so cute. That being said, most women that are true cuckoldresses but are new to the dynamic feel very awkward if they flagrantly insult their husbands. This is the man that they love and care for.

Eventually, the elephant in the room needs to be addressed. You both need to acknowledge what you both are and be ok with it. Moreover, you both need to admire and respect that your partner is the opposing and complementary side of the same equation.

You are a masochist through and through. Your wife is a sadist. You like to receive emotional and mental pain. It not only turns you on more than anything else, it also feels as natural as breathing. She likes to see you suffer. Having the ultimate power to inflict emotional pain and humiliation on you and to know you think even more of her because it is the ultimate aphrodisiac. This is the one and only 'get out of jail free' card either of you will have. Once the erotic concept of authorized infidelity wears off, you will both come to realize that that can only take your relationship so far.

Make sure you both know that cuckolding is about more than her having sex with other guys. It's a complete power transfer. It is a relationship that is unapologetically one-sided. It's a relationship that allows you both to nurture, explore and grow in a direction that you have both fought within yourselves for most of your life. I have heard of so many false start cuckold marriages that quickly come undone because they do not understand this element of the relationship by one or both people. Before you take your dirty little secret to the next level, make sure you discuss the sadistic/masochistic nature required. If there is one thing I want you to take away from this book, it's this. So many publications delve into all the deep, thick erotic sides of the wife's promiscuity but almost nowhere is it openly discussed or even mentioned that you can't have a successful cuckold marriage if you both don't independently have opposing sides of this sadomasochistic equation.

Assuming you are both still on the same page after you've discussed boundaries, expectations and acknowledged your dark sides to each other, you need to make sure you have an exit strategy for both of you. If either of you get dangerously close to doing the deed and one of you decides it's all great in the mind but not the heart, you need to have an agreed way to reverse course BEFORE things can't be undone. One word of wisdom I got on the internet when Dave introduced this all to me and I wanted to do my own research was this; Cuckolding will take a strong, healthy and loving relationship to a level outside anything you could ever possibly imagine - it did btw :). BUT, it will not fix a marriage that is already in trouble, inside or out of the bedroom. It will probably destroy it.

Sometimes, there is room for recovery, but not without some emotional scarring that takes many years to dissipate.

Chapter Eight

TESTING THE WATERS

ou should do the earliest stages of shifting to a cuckold marriage in baby steps and should be anything but real.

What?

Yup, once you are both on the same page, you need to talk, talk and then talk. Trust me, the dialogue, though informative, it's also a little like foreplay. Once you are both confident you are comfortable, start with role-playing. Perhaps consider using a dildo or toys to slowly replace you. You both need to experience your sexuality in a way that you never had as a couple. Up till this point, it's quite possible that you have never seen your partner satisfied with anyone or anything else other than yourself. Going straight to seeing another man please your wife without first experiencing her getting off on her own while you just watch will help you become familiar with emotions you may not be expecting. You want to feel natural just watching her get pleased while you either watch or listen. You also need to feel comfortable being able to please yourself as she watches. Taking these micro-steps keeps the sacredness of your marriage intact as you approach the real-world of cuckolding. There is no need to rush this. Davie and I know many couples who have skipped this step and have had disastrous consequences when the real deed is done.

You may also want to experiment with a shift in the power dynamic within your relationship. Does she struggle to take charge and demand you to her needs? Do you feel comfortable being told to please her with no reciproca-tion? Push the boundaries of emotional disparity and fair-ness in your everyday life. Have her somewhat verbally abuse you, make unfair and unrealistic demands. You want to try how it feels being used and abused (masochistic) with household chores or spending or whatever. It will also give her a chance to see if she enjoys being the Goddess that you so desperately keep claiming you feel she is. Does she like the idea of you being at her beck and call in a completely unfair context (sadism). This rather unorthodox pretest gives you both a taste of the disparity and unfairness that helps foster a beautiful loving cuckold relationship WITHOUT doing any acts that either of you may later regret. Use this time to carve out a cuck-old/cuckoldress relationship that makes you both happy, comfortable, and feeling a need to develop things to the next level.

When you both feel ready, take things up a notch. Go to a bar, club, or even a bowling alley. Let her dress like the goddess she is. Watch the heads turn her way. Are you ok with this? You want to continue pushing the envelope with each other to make sure you're both okay.

Next floor, one on one flirting. Have her eye fuck the guys across the bar. Perhaps some direct flirting as she goes to get a drink at the bar? You want to see in actual time if you are ok with the reality of her openly having eyes for another man. Once you've both have gone this far, you will instinctively know if you're heading in the right direction, and no deeds are done.

Time to take it to the ultimate level. Time for her to take the flirting and humiliation to the next level. She needs to feel comfortable having you pay for a drink to the man at the bar, making sure that he's advised it's from your wife and you. Assuming she is attracted to him, she should go over to the bar and spend most of the evening talking to him. If the opportunity arises, she should make out but end the make-out session by saying she has to return to you. I want to be clear, these step-by-step mini-tests need to be mutually devised, and agreed upon before you do anything. Up to this point, you are still working your way out of a normal vanilla relationship. The above suggestions are not to be taken as a direction you need to tell your wife what to do. Now that's funny. No, they are suggestions that I recommend you consider. My companion book for your wife also addresses similar suggestions. In no way should you be telling your wife 'do this' or 'here, do that'. It should be a joint plan to satisfy your sexual and emotional needs as a couple. If cuckolding is something you both feel naturally drawn to, this will develop with ease.

Now, after all these baby steps have been taken, you need to review and discuss how you both feel. What did she like? The freedom? The control over you? The sadistic nature of humiliating and hurting you? What did you like? What did you both not like? By now, you will both have a solid grip on where your marriage is going. You will either be excited or you discover that it best to remain a fantasy, at least for now.

Chapter Nine

BUT WHERE DO WE FIND A BULL?

o you have both talked extensively, tried to test the waters, feel comfortable and now want to take cuckolding from a concept to reality. You need a bull. A bull (assuming there may be a few readers who have been living under a rock and don't know what a bull is) is 'the other guy'.

Oh, the pain in what I'm about to tell you. Most information out there on the great interweb again glazes over this extremely challenging topic. The harsh reality is finding a magnificent bull that truly understands the dynamics of a cuckold marriage are few. I have often felt it's like I'm searching for the holy grail.

At one time Tumblr was the go-to for all alternative sex lifestyle information and hookups. Because it was largely an underground and unexploited medium, it was great. Over time, predators and parasites infiltrated Tumblr. It became a cesspool of unhealthy and frankly dangerous discussions. Tumblr eventually caught on and banned all information boards that discussed ANYTHING of a sexual nature.

Enter the specialized dating for cuckold sites. A need was there and a good deal of money-hungry predators stepped in to capitalize on good folk that just wanted to live outside the vanilla box. I tried signing up for a few of them and all I can tell you is it was a joke. The selection of bulls was pathetic. Fat, ugly, unemployed guys that lived with their mommy's seemed to be par for the course. I had davie see if he could find anyone that would fit our bill (unlike most cuckold porn, interracial matches are not mandatory for me to get excited). His memberships all required that he had to pay to sign up as a cuck, pretending to look for cuckoldresses. Suddenly, he found all these drop-dead gorgeous women that were all model material. A few IM exchanges ended abruptly when davie made it clear he was not looking for a findom. It was largely a scam for the vulnerable novice. Not to say all these sites are scams, but buyer beware.

We have had the best luck in the early stages by using local swinger clubs and websites. It would surprise you at how many swinging couples quickly evolve into cuckolding once it releases the wife from feeling shameful by having sex with other men. Swinging clubs often have theme nights with single woman (Unicorns) or single men (in our case, potential bulls). They are mostly filled with couples that want to swing, but there are often singles that are guests of the swinging couple or it's a theme night.

This kind of environment is largely hit and miss and can take several months to find a proper set of bulls that your wife is comfortable with. It does however give both you and your cuckoldress ample opportunities to more openly play to see her get intimate with other men. A word of caution here. Because these clubs are designed mostly for swinging couples, the female counterpart to the man your wife may choose to play with will expect reciprocally some playtime with yourself. I used to tell davie to just say he was my dad. It made him feel old and useless. And before you ask, yes, he loved it.

As you meet more people in any alternative lifestyle, you will develop your own network of cuck couples. The cuckoldresses share information about good bulls. Other cucks will help you in taking the final few steps to lose your old life and fully embracing cuckoldry.

Hedonism 2 is a destination resort that also has weeks throughout the year that are set for cuckold couples. Davie and I have been there several times, and it has been a blast. My problem was coming home unable to walk for a few days. I would not recommend this until you have had a chance to firmly plant your feet into the lifestyle for some time, though.

The harsh reality is there is no quick and safe entry point. Move slowly and enjoy the journey together. Each encounter will help expand and redefine your life. As you both grow, you will meet other cuck's and more importantly, your wife will begin meeting other cuckoldresses. Once this happens, you will find the transition becomes a lot more rapid and natural. You will have both refined and redefined your marriage in such a way that you will struggle with how you survived in the past with the boring world of vanilla.

Chapter Ten

OH THE PAIN...CUCKOLD ANGST

᷾

From what davie (my cucky husband) tells me, this is the very best and worst part of being a new cuckold. Make no mistake, no matter how much you think you can skip this feeling or that it won't have a colossal hit to your mind and heart, you will experience cuckold angst. It is an inevitable and good emotion.

Until it hits you the first time, you will not understand what I'm talking about. It's not nervousness or jealousy. It's not regret or anger. It's all the above magnified by a million with a twist of a massive erection that makes you feel euphoric and like you are the luckiest man in the world.

It's a very, very complicated feeling to get your head around. You feel massive amounts of emotional pain and yet you feel better than you have ever felt your entire life. This, dear readers, is the core of a cuckold. That genetic need for masochism. That longing for hurt and distress makes you feel so complete, so whole. This is where cuckold meets masochist head-on. It's these emotions you've been craving all along. You just don't recognize it yet.

With that comes a huge caveat. If you are not a cuckold at heart, this will break you in half. It will eat you up and spit you out. It is not for the faint at heart. It is for this reason alone; I have spent so much time to slow down all you anxious wannabe cucks. If you have taken the time to explore yourself, your wife and your relationship, getting to this moment will be manageable. No matter how you cut it, the first time is the absolute worst/best time that you will never forget. I don't want any man to get here and not be fully prepared.

As a bonus, every time you feel it, it will hit you at different times and different intensities and always out of nowhere. For davie, seldom shows itself until the next day. How you manage this angst is crucial. You have a melt-down and you will scare your wife so far and fast out of the lifestyle, you will never see it happen again. You both need to be aware and discuss it BEFORE it happens, so she understands you're not upset at her. My companion book tries to explain this to the wife. Why it needs to happen, why it's a wonderful thing for the cuck and how to help him deal with it.

Know that it is a natural thing and in fact, will help strengthen your relationship in the long haul. With each time you feel cuck angst, you begin to feel more comfort-able and learn to embrace it as part of what you crave. You realize this is something you need to make you whole. It's not a bad thing. Your wife also learns to spread her wings and embrace the sadistic side of herself. As she grows as a cuckoldress, she will recognize the value of you feeling this pain and proactively find ways to ensure and intensify the feeling.

Your wife may take some time to feel comfortable in her own skin being a cuckoldress that humiliates while she's fucking another guy, yet still, maintain a balance of love and care for you. Likewise, you too will need to be gentle on yourself. You will need to accept it will take time to feel comfortable feeling angst. Your head will say NO! But your heart will say MORE! As the cliche goes, what the heart wants, the heart always gets.

Chapter Eleven

SETTLING IN - YOUR NEW LIFE

f you have read this far, I suspect I have struck a chord. Deep inside you know this is a life that you not only crave, it feels as natural as breathing. It is not something you want to do, it's something you are and will always be.

First, congratulations! You have come out of the closet, smashed society's stereotypes of what a marriage is supposed to be like, and have been true to yourself. You have carved a path that is right for you. Have confidence that you are living a dynamic that many fantasize about, but very few have the guts to live. You will both have exponential growth in the early stages. Pushing boundaries, setting new ones. You may find you initially did not want your wife to play without you being there, but now feel not only comfortable with it, you also love the idea of her meeting a bull after work. It will give you extra time to finish the laundry and make a delightful meal for her arrival.

It's usually at this stage in your cuckold life where female-led relationships and cuckolding meet. The cuckold marriage starts with sexual motivations and moves into shifting power dynamics outside the bedroom. Female-led relationships start with a shift in the power dynamic and then take it to the bedroom. The problem with starting with an FLR ahead of cuckolding is the possibility that one of you may in no way be interested in cuckolding. This sets up for a long journey where one or both become very dissatisfied. Starting with cuckolding and moving to a Female Led Relationship is inevitable.

Understand that a cuckold marriage is a completely sadomasochistic relationship where the pain/pleasure is derived in the mind, not physically. Additionally, the roles are never, ever reversed. This seems to always be the core component of cuckolding that always gets fluffed over and never really addressed head-on. Knowing this upfront and in advance, I think makes the entire transition a lot easier and clear.

The disparity grows to a level you are both comfortable with. No more, no less. Where that line is will take several years. Davie and I have been in this life for over seven years, and it took us at least 4 years to get it right.

Unlike most marriages, cuckolding requires the couple to openly admit the ugliest side of themselves (at least as judged by the vanilla world) and have their partner completely accept, embrace, admire and prefer this side. Where the magic happens is that it works in both directions.

She loves to fuck, often. She wants to be a slut but has

repressed, perhaps even buried it her entire life. She enjoys being a bad girl and gets a kick out of making you her little cuckyboy. Most importantly, she loves that you are not only okay with her being this way; you worship her BECAUSE of it.

You love the idea of your wife being a sex god to all men. You can think of no better way to live than by her being in complete charge of your sexuality. You love that she has a dark side and worship her when she tells you that your little pee pee is cute but that she needs a real man.

This combined, mutual and complementary mindset creates a bond that is indescribable and unmatched by almost any conventional relationship I'm aware of. However, don't think this kind of relationship is only about sex and all things cuckolding. We still have much time where there is a soft loving and giving to each other. The point of opening a pandora's box of cuckoldry into your marriage is to enrich and expand. To openly allow both of you to grow in ways that society tells us we can't. But the important thing to remember is the love you have for each other is paramount. Lose that and it's over.

Schedule "off days" where the cuck dynamic is paused. You need humiliation and angst, but you also need to know you're wanted and loved. She needs control and ecstasy, but she also needs to know and feel you are her man with authentic emotions and needs and not just her play toy.

As I said at the beginning of this book, cuckoldry is not for everyone. It is, in my opinion, the most rewarding and exciting relationship anyone could be in. It is also the most challenging and potentially volatile. It is not for the faint of heart. You can not enter this kind of life and not already have a rock-solid foundation for your marriage. It will not fix a poor sex life, nor will it bring an already distant couple closer together. You need to have both those elements in place, BEFOREHAND. Cuckolding simply takes all this goodness to the next level.

Chapter Twelve

MAINTENANCE FOR THE LONGHAUL

꧁

I wanted to end this book with a question davie and I get asked all the time from some of our swinging couple friends. "How long can you last doing cuckolding before your marriage falls apart?"

The truth is FOREVER.

You being an emotional masochist and your wife being a sadist at heart. Both of you feeding each other sexually in opposing ways. It is a true match made in heaven. I truly mean you should be together. Cuckoldry cements a closeness way deeper than any average relationship.

As I've already mentioned, a cuckold marriage is arguably the most satisfying and rewarding marriage possible. Unfortunately, it also is the most turbulent and challenging. No matter how hard you try, you will have issues with each other. She will not feel "in the mood" when you are craving to see her ride the pony hard. You may struggle with a bout of angst and need additional time to resolve your pain while she is itching to go out with her new bull and have her brains fucked out. She may feel guilty about being exceptionally cruel to you as she fucks her bull and tells you your cock is a joke. You may resent her for being sensitive and caring about your pain and would rather have her tell you to suck it up, princess.

The key is honesty and communication. You both need to maintain a constant stream of conversation when any issues bubble up, and they will. Cuckoldry is not a destination. It's a journey. Just like your job, your place of residence, the price of gas or the weather. It is constantly changing. Your expectations, your emotional buttons, your need for reassurance that you are still loved. All of them will shift by degrees as you move forward.

Because you have both openly shared a side of you that society deeply suppresses, it opens a door of closeness, love and understanding that transcends most vanilla relationships. It becomes your dirty little secret that feels magical. But it can quickly be forgotten or overlooked once you both spend more time immersed in cuckolding.

Try to imagine going your whole life hiding that you accidentally burned your parents' house down as a child. You suppress the guilt and shame and swear to never tell a soul. You then discover your best friend did the same thing when they were a child. Discovering that you're not alone. That you can finally talk to another human about it and not be judged puts the closeness and openness you feel to that person at a level you thought not possible. Not the best example here, but the knowledge that you can now go on and know you're not alone is extremely powerful. You just can't forget that this special bond is in a very sensitive area of specialness. More often than not, your partner cannot share their fears, concerns, or annoyances with too many other people. You're likely one of the few people they can dump on. The problem is, it's about you they want to dump.

Being able to be your true self and be able to comfortably admit you like to be humiliated and degraded with the response by your wife as "cool, I like to humiliate, manipulate and I'm glad for you being ok that I'm kind of a slut". This all happens BEFORE you get this far. Now you have to maintain the dialogue.

Are you feeling insecure cause she wants to keep hooking up with the same bull repeatedly? Are you feeling like she is too stern using a cock cage for a full month? Is she feeling repressed because she wants to play more than once a week and you're too tired to drive her to the club? Perhaps she is feeling like you are not obedient enough and it's really important to her to see you on clean-up duty after she visits with a bull?

Now that you're in the thick of cuckolding, the need to communicate often can be easily forgotten. Moreover, you can find things become routinized and standards get set with no discussion. Both of you need to be aware of this little dip and have scheduled 'check-up' meetings regularly, to ensure you're always connected in both the mind and soul.

Take a minute to appreciate how your weakest and ugliest sides (as stereotyped by society) are revered by your spouse. A whole new level of bonding takes place here guys. Trust me. Once I told davie that I loved the idea of calling him my princess, and he thought more of me if I was a slut. OMG! I'm getting wet just thinking about that. Sorry.

I have put together a companion book for wives. It deals exclusively with all the questions, concerns, and advice I've had to learn the hard way as a cuckoldress. It will help her understand how you tick, what cuckolding is REALLY about-She just won the lottery but doesn't know it yet. It will help her look at her own self-diagnosis and break through the guilt she may feel by acknowledging she has needs that are not being met. It will assist her in figuring out if this is a life that may be an ideal fit for her as well, or she may find she is too submissive to even explore it. I strongly encourage you to have her check it out.

Anyway, as with any relationship, understand that you can not just take things for granted. EVER! Especially in this dynamic. Keep talking, keep tweaking. Yes, this is an unconventional way to go through life, but if it makes you both happy, why the hell would you not?

*K*isses,
A. xo

THE JOURNEY CONTINUES

Available Feb 2nd, 2021 - Groundhog Day!

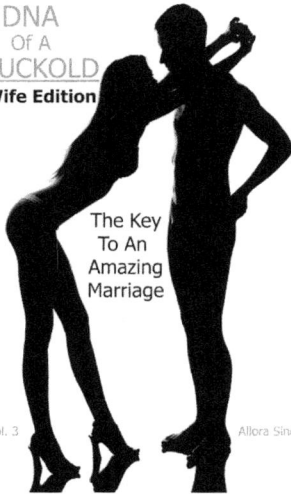

DNA
Of A
CUCKOLD
Wife Edition

The Key
To An
Amazing
Marriage

Vol. 3   Allora Sinclair

A complimentary book geared directly to wives. A gentle breakdown helping them understand their husband, why it actually makes sense and assessing if it's in their own DNA. The ideal ice breaker for those who want to be on the same page when the topic finally gets discussed.

TESTIMONIALS

Stacey and Eric

"We have learned to accept each other for who we really are. Allora has been a wonderful inspiration to help us grow our cuckold love."

☿

Belinda and Derek

"I thought we understood cuckolding after 3 years. Allora's books have proven us wrong. This has really helped us move forward and grow as a couple."

☿

Robert

"No more guilt. Reading her (A. Sinclair) book has taken a huge weight off my shoulders. I'm not broken. My wife is exited about reading her next book."

Kim and Amed

"Detailed, concise and calling it as it really is. My cucky and I thank you Ms. Sinclair. You have saved our marriage."

ALSO BY ALLORA SINCLAIR

ABOUT THE AUTHOR

Allora Sinclair is a happily married 40 year old. She and her loving cuckold husband Dave (davie) have been in a cuckold marriage for over seven years and she has now decided to start documenting their journey from vanilla to a complete FLR relationship. If Allora is not found at her computer or out shopping for shoes, she is usually found in the caring arms of davie or embraced in ecstasy with one of her favourite bulls. She has done a series of non-fiction books to help couples navigate their way through the heavily distorted life of being a cuckold couple. She is now working on a series of fiction books that are based on some of their real-life experiences. If you like what she's doing, please leave a review wherever you purchased this book.